SABBATH

THE GIFT
OF REST

LYNNE
M. BAAB

8 STUDIES
FOR INDIVIDUALS
OR GROUPS

Life
Builder
Study

INTER-VARSITY PRESS
36 Causton Street, London SW1P 4ST, England
Email: ivp@ivpbooks.com
Website: www.ivpbooks.com

Originally published in the United States of America in the LifeGuide® Bible Studies series in 2007 by InterVarsity Press, Downers Grove, Illinois
First published in Great Britain in 2018

British Library Cataloguing-in-Publication Data
A catalogue record for this book is available from the British Library

ISBN: 978–1–78359–704–8
eBook ISBN: 978–1–78359–705–5

Inter-Varsity Press publishes Christian books that are true to the Bible and that communicate the gospel, develop discipleship and strengthen the church for its mission in the world.

IVP originated within the Inter-Varsity Fellowship, now the Universities and Colleges Christian Fellowship, a student movement connecting Christian Unions in universities and colleges throughout Great Britain, and a member movement of the International Fellowship of Evangelical Students. Website: www.uccf.org.uk. That historic association is maintained, and all senior IVP staff and committee members subscribe to the UCCF Basis of Faith.

Contents

Getting the Most Out of *Sabbath*

Sabbath is not an everyday term in our culture. What is the sabbath? A weekly day of rest and worship. A day to rejoice in abundance. A day to practice thankfulness. A day to slow down, take a deep breath, step aside from work and worries, and let the world go on without us, knowing that God is caring for everyone and everything.

In the midst of the stress of juggling and multitasking, keeping the sabbath brings simplicity and a sense of God's peace. More people of all ages are finding the sabbath to be a gift from God that brings a renewed awareness of who God is and who we are as God's beloved children.

The sabbath was one of the distinctive marks of God's people in the Bible. The other nations labored seven days a week, but the Jews rested from work one day out of seven. On that day, they remembered that God created the world and rested on the seventh day. They also remembered that God freed them from slavery in Egypt. The day of rest was a sign of God's goodness to them as Creator and Redeemer.

Jesus observed the sabbath day. Several Gospel stories show him worshiping in the synagogue. Early followers of Jesus kept the Jewish sabbath on Saturday and celebrated Christ's resurrection on Sundays, which they called "the Lord's Day." Over time, as Christianity spread among people who weren't Jewish, Sundays became the weekly day that was set apart from the other days. On that day, Christians remembered Jesus' resurrection, rested from work if possible, and participated in worship with others.

In the second half of the twentieth century, this day of rest was largely lost. Because of the increasing pace of life, many people today are experiencing a renewed interest in finding rhythms of rest. The biblical sabbath pattern has much to teach us about how and why to rest, and how to keep God at the center of a day of rest.

How Do We Practice Sabbath?

In order to begin observing the sabbath, two questions must be considered. First, *what will I stop doing on the sabbath?* Options for things to stop include: paid work, housework, home repairs, money management, shopping, answering e-mail or watching TV.

The second question to consider is *what will I do on the sabbath to draw near to God?* The danger in this second question is that we may have such high and idealistic expectations for spiritual significance on our sabbath day that we miss the main point. According to the *New Bible Dictionary* the Hebrew root meaning of the word *sabbath* is "to cease" or "to desist."* In ceasing or stopping, we acknowledge that God is God and we are not. In stopping work, we act out the truth that everything we have comes from God, not our own effort. The sabbath provides a structure for us to respond to God's invitation: "Be still, and know that I am God" (Psalm 46:10).

Still, sabbath keepers today engage in a variety of practices on the sabbath to enable them to draw near to God: festive family meals, getting out in nature, journaling, Bible study, prayer, reading poetry, enjoying art and music, or even the simple discipline of breathing deeply.

In this study guide, we will consider biblical passages that provide a background for many sabbath practices. A restful and Christ-centered sabbath grows out of embracing a *small* number of activities on the sabbath and doing them in an intentional, peaceful and joyful manner.

Each study in this guide will give an opportunity to consider what you might stop doing on the sabbath in order to make space for God. You will also be invited to consider what activities you might do on the sabbath to nurture intimacy with God. Each study focuses on a different aspect of the sabbath; over the course of the eight studies you will explore a variety of things you might *stop* doing on the sabbath and a variety of things you might *do* on the sabbath.

If you desire to start a sabbath observance, watch your reactions to

---

*I. Howard Marshall, A. R. Millard, J. I. Packer and Donald J. Wiseman, eds., *New Bible Dictionary* (Leicester: IVP, 1996), p. 1032.

the eight studies. Notice which studies resonate most deeply with you, and pay particular attention to the things you name in each of those studies that you might stop doing or begin doing on the sabbath.

After you have finished all eight studies pick one to three things to stop doing and one to three things to start doing. Begin small; don't start with a long list! Then implement your plan for three to six months without analyzing the plan's "effectiveness." Just enjoy the sabbath day and let it teach you. After three to six months, then evaluate and decide if you want to try some other things.

Your sabbath can be any day of the week. For most Christians, Sundays work best because attending worship helps us focus on God. Some Christians come from a tradition with a Saturday sabbath. Some of us work on Saturdays or Sundays and need to pick another day. In these studies you will gain an overview of God's priorities for the sabbath, and you will be able to make good choices for your own sabbath. All of these studies center around God's wonderful call to rediscover a gift that brings spiritual refreshment and refocusing.

Suggestions for Individual Study

1. As you begin each study, pray that God will speak to you through his Word.

2. Read the introduction to the study and respond to the personal reflection question or exercise. This is designed to help you focus on God and on the theme of the study.

3. Each study deals with a particular passage—so that you can delve into the author's meaning in that context. Read and reread the passage to be studied. The questions are written using the language of the New International Version, so you may wish to use that version of the Bible. The New Revised Standard Version is also recommended.

4. This is an inductive Bible study, designed to help you discover for yourself what Scripture is saying. The study includes three types of questions. *Observation* questions ask about the basic facts: who, what, when, where and how. *Interpretation* questions delve into the meaning of the passage. *Application* questions help you discover the implications of the text for growing in Christ. These three keys unlock the treasures of Scripture.

Write your answers to the questions in the spaces provided or in a personal journal. Writing can bring clarity and deeper understanding of yourself and of God's Word.

5. It might be good to have a Bible dictionary handy. Use it to look up any unfamiliar words, names or places.

6. Use the prayer suggestion to guide you in thanking God for what you have learned and to pray about the applications that have come to mind.

7. You may want to go on to the suggestion under "Now or Later," or you may want to use that idea for your next study.

Suggestions for Members of a Group Study

1. Come to the study prepared. Follow the suggestions for individual study mentioned above. You will find that careful preparation will greatly enrich your time spent in group discussion.

2. Be willing to participate in the discussion. The leader of your group will not be lecturing. Instead, he or she will be encouraging the members of the group to discuss what they have learned. The leader will be asking the questions that are found in this guide.

3. Stick to the topic being discussed. Your answers should be based on the verses which are the focus of the discussion and not on outside authorities such as commentaries or speakers. These studies focus on a particular passage of Scripture. Only rarely should you refer to other portions of the Bible. This allows for everyone to participate in in-depth study on equal ground.

4. Be sensitive to the other members of the group. Listen attentively when they describe what they have learned. You may be surprised by their insights! Each question assumes a variety of answers. Many questions do not have "right" answers, particularly questions that aim at meaning or application. Instead the questions push us to explore the passage more thoroughly.

When possible, link what you say to the comments of others. Also, be affirming whenever you can. This will encourage some of the more hesitant members of the group to participate.

5. Be careful not to dominate the discussion. We are sometimes so eager to express our thoughts that we leave too little opportunity for others to respond. By all means participate! But allow others to also.

6. Expect God to teach you through the passage being discussed and through the other members of the group. Pray that you will have an enjoyable and profitable time together, but also that as a result of the study you will find ways that you can take action individually and/or as a group.

7. Remember that anything said in the group is considered confidential and should not be discussed outside the group unless specific permission is given to do so.

8. If you are the group leader, you will find additional suggestions at the back of the guide.

1

An Invitation to Relax in Abundance

Genesis 1:1—2:3

Six days a week we wrestle with the world,
wringing profit from the earth; on the Sabbath we especially
care for the seed of eternity planted in the soul. The world has our
hands, but our soul belongs to Someone Else.

ABRAHAM HESCHEL

God made an incredibly beautiful and abundant world. Because the world is fallen, we can see brokenness and pain all around us. We can see what is missing, and we work and pray to help restore creation to its intended wholeness. On the sabbath we are invited to set aside our concern for what is missing in our lives. We are invited to stop working and simply rest in the good and wonderful aspects of everything God has given us.

The sabbath is a day to rest from work and thoughts of work, because we remember that God created the world and that God rested after creation. In the Jewish tradition, the sabbath is also a day to rest from the work of intercessory prayer. On the sabbath, appropriate prayers are prayers of thankfulness. Expressing thanks helps us notice the beauty of God's world and the many ways God is at work in the world.

GROUP DISCUSSION. On a piece of paper write down five recent events or aspects of your life for which you are particularly grateful. Describe to the group one thing you wrote down, and explain the ways that event or aspect of your life speaks to you of God's goodness and generosity.

PERSONAL REFLECTION. In what ways and in what settings do you experience God's generosity and goodness? What impedes your experience of God's generosity and goodness?

We will examine the beautifully constructed account of God's creation of the world. *Read Genesis 1:1—2:3.*

---

1. In Genesis 1:2 how is the earth described?

---

2. Study the description of the six days of creation (1:3-31). What is the role of God's voice?

---

3. What patterns are repeated in the descriptions of each of the six days?

---

4. What aspects of the sixth day (vv. 24-31) were "very good" in contrast to the other five days?

5. In the description of the six days, what words and phrases communicate abundance?

6. Compare 1:2 and 2:1, the "before and after" descriptions of creation. In what ways do the words of 2:1 contribute to our understanding of the abundance and order of creation?

7. In what ways do the abundance and order of the creation speak to you of God's character?

8. Note the repetition of the words *work* and *rest* in 2:2-3. Richard Lowery writes, "In a delightful twist, 'rest' is a verb in this passage and 'work' is a noun."* What does this tell you about the nature of this rest?

9. What are some of the possible reasons God rested after creating the world?

10. In 2:3 we also find the key words *blessed* and *holy*. What do the words *blessed* and *holy* mean to you?

11. What activities in your life tend to narrow your ability to see God's abundance and order in your life?

What would it look like to stop one or more of these activities on the sabbath?

12. What activities help you notice the abundance that God has given you?

Which of these activities can you imagine incorporating into a sabbath observance?

Spend some time thanking God for the abundant world he created. Ask God to open your eyes to see the signs of abundance in your own life.

Now or Later

Psalm 104 parallels the creation story in a beautiful way. The same themes of order and abundance are present, and God is portrayed as the One who cares for and sustains creation. Read Psalm 104 twice, slowly. The first time, absorb the details and descriptions in the psalm, noticing what the psalmist is saying about the ways God works in the creation. The second time you read the psalm, use the words as your prayer of adoration of the Creator. Spend some time thinking about the ways you could rest in God's order and abundance on the sabbath.

*Richard Lowery, Sabbath and Jubilee (St. Louis, Mo.: Chalice Press, 2000), p. 93.

2

Choosing to Stop Working

Exodus 16:1-30

*Celebration of our special time together with God recharges us
and fills us with energy to meet the demands of the coming
week—much like a short break from our work.
You know how it happens—you're hard at work but so tired
that your productivity starts to slide backward.
So you get up from your desk, maybe chat with a neighbor down
the hall, get a drink from the water cooler, and stretch your legs. When
you return to your work, you catch your second wind
and go right on. The Sabbath is the jewel of the week. Spending the
set-apart time hours of the Sabbath with God gives us our second wind.*

CELESTE PERRINO WALKER

People who have kept the sabbath steadily over a period of time
report that they get more done in six days than they ever got done in
seven. For the people I interviewed, the motivation to keep the sabbath came not out of the potential increased productivity but from a
desire to honor God and receive from God the gift of rest. However,
increased productivity comes as a sabbath gift because humans seem
to have been created for a rhythm of six days of work and one day of
rest. The day of rest gives a sense of direction and purpose—a time for

refocusing—that makes work flow more easily on the six days of work.

GROUP DISCUSSION. On a piece of paper write down one thing you like about working (either work for pay or doing tasks at home) and one thing you like about taking a break from work. Describe to the group one thing you wrote down, and explain why you like it.

PERSONAL REFLECTION. What do you like about feeling productive? How do you feel on a day when you are not productive? Does feeling productive ever feel addictive to you?

In this passage we will look at the earliest sabbath observance by God's people, right after the Israelites were freed from slavery in Egypt. *Read Exodus 16:1-30.*

1. In verses 1-12, what do you learn about the grumbling of the Israelites?

2. In what kinds of situations are you tempted to grumble?

3. What does God promise in response to the Israelites' grumbling (vv. 4, 5 and 11-12)?

4. Describe the outcome of God's promises (vv. 13-21).

5. What are the specific instructions about gathering manna on the seventh day (vv. 5, 22-26)?

What miraculous properties of manna made these instructions possible?

6. Describe any times when you have obeyed God and then found that small miracles followed.

7. What are some of the thoughts and feelings that might have motivated the people to try to gather manna on the seventh day (vv. 27-30)?

8. What was God's response to their action?

9. What does this story teach us about God?

10. In what settings and in the midst of what activities do you find it hard to remember God is your provider?

Take a few moments to reflect. What would it look like to stop some of those activities on the sabbath?

---

11. What helps you remember that God is your provider?

What might it look like to incorporate some of those activities into a sabbath observance?

Spend some time thanking God for his miracles and for being your provider.

Now or Later

Three Old Testament verses help us understand God's gift of rest, quiet and stillness that we receive on the sabbath: Psalm 46:10; Isaiah 30:15; and Jeremiah 6:16. Read these verses and look for the promises or blessings connected with slowing down. Spend some time praying or journaling about the obstacles in your life to receiving these promises or blessings.

Reflect on these words: "Sabbath affirms the dignity of all people. When no one is working, it is hard to tell the difference between them by their achievements. They are equal as imagebearers of God, as persons loved by God! So sabbath is a sign of divine grace, a reminder of who we are before God. We have value beyond what we produce or achieve. In fact, we are accepted by God before we do or achieve anything important."*

---

*Donald Postema, *Catch Your Breath* (Grand Rapids: CRC Publications, 1997), p. 66.

3

Finding Refreshment in God's Creation

Exodus 20:1-21

"Sabbath is more than the absence of work; it is not just a day off, when we catch up on television or errands. It is the presence of something that arises when we consecrate a period of time to listen to what is most deeply beautiful, nourishing, or true. It is time consecrated with our attention, our mindfulness, honoring those quiet forces of grace or spirit that sustain and heal us."

WAYNE MULLER

Many sabbath-keepers enjoy experiencing God's creation on their day of rest. Noticing and appreciating the handiwork of the Artist gives joy, peace and a sense of perspective about everyday life. Focusing on God as Creator can help us let go of responsibility and productivity one day each week because God is in charge of the universe.

GROUP DISCUSSION. On a piece of paper, write down five places in nature where you have experienced God's presence. Describe to the group one of those places, and explain the ways you have heard God's voice or experienced God's reality in that place.

PERSONAL REFLECTION. In what ways do places in nature speak to you of God's character and love? Thank God for the beauty of creation and the ways you have experienced God's voice there.

We will begin this study with an overview of the giving of the Ten Commandments. *Read Exodus 20:1-21.*

---

1. Verses 2-17 list the Ten Commandments. What areas of everyday life are covered in these commands?

---

2. Verses 18-21 describe the people's response and Moses' encouragement not to be fearful. Imagine that you are there. What are you thinking and feeling?

---

3. Focus on verses 8-11. Verse 8 commands that we remember the sabbath day and keep it holy. What kinds of practices help you to experience holiness?

---

4. Verse 10 tells us that work and labor are forbidden on the sabbath. What similar and different meanings do the two words—work and labor—communicate to you?

What emotions do you feel when you hear the words *work* and *labor*?

5. Exodus 35:3 forbids lighting a fire on the sabbath. Consider what it takes to build a fire and the kinds of work that depend on having a fire lit. In your life, what kinds of activities are work?

6. In verse 10 look at the list of who is commanded to stop working. Whose inclusion in this list do you find surprising, and what, if anything, does that tell you about who or what God values/honors?

7. When we fail to practice the sabbath, would you say that we are disregarding one of God's commandments? Why or why not?

8. God's model of resting at creation is the basis for the sabbath command (v. 11). What helps you remember that God is our Creator?

9. When you experience God as Creator, in what ways are you refreshed?

10. On the sabbath what is one thing you might stop doing in order to remember that God is Creator?

---

11. What is one thing you might do to experience God as Creator?

Spend some time thanking God for the beauty of creation and for the ways you experience this reality in your life.

Now or Later

Deuteronomy 5:12-15 gives a longer version of the sabbath command that comes from late in Moses' life. In this version, the reason for keeping the sabbath comes from the fact that God freed the Israelites from slavery. The *New Bible Dictionary* states that this amplified reason for the commandment might be a natural expression of a fluent speaker who had been talking about the Ten Commandments to God's people for many years. Christians affirm that we have been freed from slavery to sin and death (Galatians 4:3-8). Read Deuteronomy 5:12-15, then compare and contrast it with Exodus 20:1-21. Consider the ways the sabbath command in Deuteronomy rounds out your understanding of the sabbath.

4

Discovering Sabbath Delight

If our worship is authentic, it will reveal God's mercy.
This awareness qualifies our actions on Sunday.
It leads us to reflect the mercy that led Jesus to heal on the sabbath,
and early Christians and the church thereafter to speak of
'works of mercy' on Sunday as appropriate activities.

TILDEN EDWARDS

Sam, a writer for an advertising agency, has been keeping sabbath for several years. He used to bring work home on Sundays, particularly when he couldn't see how he could meet his deadlines without adding in some Sunday hours. Now he always refrains from working on Sundays. Ever since he's been keeping the sabbath, he has enjoyed watching God perform small miracles that enable him to get his tasks at work done on time, even when human logic tells him he needs those Sunday work hours to meet a deadline.

Sam keeps the sabbath because it is commanded in the Ten Commandments, but there is nothing rigid or legalistic about his obedience. He experiences a greater sense of partnership with God in his work because of keeping the sabbath holy. Sam would be the first to suggest that keeping the sabbath is a blessing to us, not an onerous duty based on rigid rules. And he would also say that the sabbath is a part of a life of faith, truly a delight.

GROUP DISCUSSION. Think of a spiritual discipline or practice you have engaged in that felt like "going through the motions." Or think of a spiritual discipline or practice that, over time, brought good fruit in your life. (Some examples of spiritual disciplines or practices are praying, reading the Bible, going to church, tithing, fasting and keeping the sabbath.) Drawing from your experiences, describe the characteristics of a healthy or unhealthy spiritual practice.

PERSONAL REFLECTION. Look back at the disciplines that have shaped you over time, such as spiritual practices (prayer, tithing, Scripture reading) or habits (exercising, tracking finances). What are the characteristics of disciplines that bring good things in your life?

In this study, fasting and sabbath keeping are two examples of spiritual disciplines. *Read Isaiah 58.*

1. What is the nature of the "rebellion" and "sins" of the people described in verses 1-5?

What key words and phrases describe this rebellion and sin?

2. In verses 6-10, what does God desire to be the characteristics of the fast he chooses?

3. What visual images are used in verses 8, 11 and 12?

In what ways do these images speak to you personally?

———————————————————————————

4. Summarize all the statements in verses 9, 10 and 13 that begin with "if."

———————————————————————————

5. What would these conditions look like in practice?

Which of them are hardest for you to imagine doing?

———————————————————————————

6. Verse 14 expresses three promises that result from keeping the sabbath with honor. Imagine those promises had been written today. What might they say?

7. Fasting and sabbath keeping are two examples of spiritual disciplines. Based on the instructions in this passage about these two practices, what are some of God's priorities for us when we exercise spiritual disciplines?

8. Can you see possible connections between the practice of justice in your daily life and delight on the sabbath day? Explain your response.

9. In what ways and in what settings are you most tempted to "do as you please"(vv. 3, 13) or "go your own way" (v. 13) while seeming to engage in a spiritual discipline or practice?

What activities that encourage you to "do as you please" or "go your own way" might you stop on the sabbath?

10. In what settings do you most experience delight in God?

11. What activities might you stop doing or start doing on the sabbath in order to "call the sabbath a delight" and "honorable" (v. 13)?

Ask God to help you avoid going your own way and doing as you please while seeming to engage in spiritual practices.

Now or Later

The book of Amos focuses on the same themes as Isaiah 58. Amos expresses God's desire that the people of Israel care for the poor and needy. Amos also describes God's disgust with religious practices that focus on form rather than substance. Read Amos 5:21-24 and 8:4-8, the most succinct parallels with Isaiah 58. (You may also enjoy reading Amos 2:6-8; 4:1-5; 5:6-15; and 6:1-8.) Spend some time praying or journaling about the connection between justice in everyday life and the spiritual disciplines or practices we engage in.

5

A Gift for Us

Mark 2:23-28

*The Pharisees see sabbath observance as a sign of
cultural distinctiveness and cultic purity.
Jesus sees sabbath as a sign of justice for the vulnerable poor.*

RICHARD LOWERY

My Grandpa Ray was born in the 1890s. He had eight older sisters and a very strict father. After church and the big family meal on Sunday at noon, Ray's father allowed only two activities for the rest of the day: sitting still or reading the Bible. The eight girls in the family managed to comply, but for Ray those Sunday afternoons and evenings were torture, following too close after the torture of sitting still in church on Sunday mornings. Ray seldom attended church as an adult.

GROUP DISCUSSION. Think back on a time that you received a gift and the giver expressed conditions about where and how the gift could or could not be used. How did you react? How did you feel?

PERSONAL REFLECTION. Reflect on the best gifts you have received. What are the characteristics of gifts that truly communicate love?

In this story, Jesus discusses the purpose of the sabbath. *Read Mark 2:23-28.*

---

1. Use your imagination to try to picture the setting of this story. Who is present and where are they?

---

2. Summarize Jesus' response to the Pharisees' question (vv. 25-26).

---

3. Read 1 Samuel 21:1-6, the incident Jesus refers to in verses 25 and 26. What are the similarities and differences between this incident involving David and Jesus' confrontation with the Pharisees in Mark 2:23-28?

---

4. How do you respond to the idea that human hunger and need are more important in some situations than obeying the rules?

What do you think should be the limits around breaking rules to meet human needs?

5. Consider Jesus' statement in Mark 2:27. In a culture where rigid sabbath rules were the norm, in what ways would this be a radical statement?

6. Imagine that God has created a day just for you, to nurture intimacy between you and God and to enable you to be your best self, the person you were created to be. What would that day look like?

7. Jesus says he is Lord of the sabbath. How might his disciples have responded to that statement?

How might the Pharisees have responded?

8. In what ways does Jesus, as Lord of the sabbath, seem to be redefining the meaning of the day?

9. Consider what it means in everyday life that Jesus is Lord. What connections can you see between allowing Jesus to be Lord and receiving the sabbath as a gift from God?

10. What activities help you honor Jesus as Lord?

Which of those activities could you do on the sabbath?

11. What activities feel like a gift from God?

How could you incorporate one or more of these into your sabbath observance?

Spend some time thanking God for his many gifts. Pray your own prayer of submission to Jesus as your Lord.

Now or Later

Psalm 139 focuses on the fact that God knows us inside and out. Read Psalm 139:1-18 two times slowly, the first time to absorb the contents of the psalm. The second time, pray the words of the psalm as you read them, using the words as a way to praise God for his intimate knowledge of you. Consider ways you might rest on the sabbath, enjoying the fact that God knows you and gives you good things in your life based on his knowledge of you.

6

We Are Valuable

*Jesus made it a point to act against the prevailing tradition
by healing on the Sabbath. He did it deliberately, not in defiance
of the very real obligations of the Sabbath commandment but
in order to restore the day to what God intended it to be.
The people He healed were chronically ill, in bondage to Satan
physically and spiritually. By offering them physical and
spiritual liberation, He made the Sabbath a time to celebrate and
experience the blessing of his redemptive ministry.
His message to us, then and now, is that we are a saved, free people!*
CELESTE PERRINO WALKER

People who have kept a sabbath for many years differ in what they do and don't do on this day of rest. One couple enjoys fixing a leisurely breakfast as a sign of the abundance of time on this day. A college student enjoys wearing a dress to church. She stays in the dress all day to set the day apart from other days. Many people keep the computer and TV off, as a sign that there is more to life than the pressure of e-mail and the lure of entertainment. We are of infinite value in God's eyes, and our actions, large and small, on the sabbath can engrave in our hearts that we are not merely machines of productivity. We are beloved children of God.

GROUP DISCUSSION. On a piece of paper, write down five things you think God values about you. Describe to the group something you wrote down. Why do you think we find it so hard to believe we are valued in God's eyes?

PERSONAL REFLECTION. In what settings do you experience the reality that God views you as infinitely valuable? In what settings do you find it hard to believe God values you? What are the differences between the two kinds of settings?

This study focuses on a dramatic encounter between Jesus, a man with a shriveled hand and a group of Pharisees. *Read Matthew 12:9-14.*

1. Why would the Pharisees ask a question about the sabbath in order to trap Jesus?

2. What do we know about the man with the shriveled hand?

3. Imagine you were a bystander watching this incident. What do you think you would notice most clearly about the Pharisees?

4. Study the story in verses 11-12. What is the difference between planned and unplanned work on the sabbath?

5. What are the similarities and differences between the sheep story and the healing of the man's hand?

6. What do you think doing good on the sabbath might look like in our lives?

7. Jesus asserts that people are much more valuable than sheep (v. 12). How is it possible to affirm the value of humans in God's eyes without demeaning the value of sheep and other creatures God created?

8. Why do you think the Pharisees wanted to kill Jesus after this incident?

9. Based on this passage, what can you say about the purpose of the sabbath?

10. Jesus affirmed how valuable people are. What activities make it hard for you to remember how valuable you are in God's eyes?

What would it look like to stop doing one or more of those activities on the sabbath?

_____

11. What activities help you remember how valuable and precious you are in God's eyes?

Perhaps you have been experimenting with new activities on the sabbath. In what ways do they help you remember you are valuable and precious to God?

Spend some time praying about the obstacles to believing you are precious and valued in God's eyes.

Now or Later

In both Matthew and Mark, the story from this lesson follows immediately after the story from study five (Matthew 12:1-14 and Mark 2:23—3:6). In both gospels, the verses before and after these sabbath incidents can add to our understanding of God's gift of the sabbath to us. Read the two sabbath stories in their contexts and see what additional perspectives on the sabbath you can gain (Matthew 11:25—12:21 and Mark 2:23—3:6).

7

Freed from Bondage

When we keep a sabbath holy, we are practicing,
for a day, the freedom that God intends for all people.
We are practicing life outside the frantic pace set by financial markets
and round-the-clock shopping and entertainment venues.
We are practicing independence from the forces of injustice.
We are trying on a new way of life as we begin to allow our weeks
to be changed in response to God's promises.

DOROTHY BASS

The sabbath is a day to experience freedom. Do you tend to worry too much? Do you dislike the way your body looks? Stopping worrying or engaging in negative thoughts may be too much to attempt seven days a week, but it might be possible for one day. Do you get weary of the tasks of daily life—mowing the lawn, balancing the checkbook, doing the dishes, exercising regularly? We cannot ignore those tasks seven days a week, but for one day each week, we can set many of them aside and experience freedom.

GROUP DISCUSSION. How would you define freedom? What kinds of freedom do you experience in your daily life? What kinds of freedom do you long to experience?

PERSONAL REFLECTION. Think back on times you have experienced what you consider to be true freedom. What did it look like? feel like?

In what ways was God present in that experience of freedom?

In this story we will see Jesus set a woman free. *Read Luke 13:10-17.*

---

1. Imagine you are the woman who is bent over. What might have been some of the challenges you faced in your daily life over the past eighteen years?

What might be some of your emotions before, during and after Jesus healed you?

---

2. Why do you think the synagogue rulers were indignant about this healing?

---

3. Consider the synagogue rulers' words in verse 14. Do you think they really would have preferred that Jesus heal on weekdays? Why or why not?

4. What is the main point of the comparison with giving water to an ox or donkey on the sabbath?

5. Why is being set free an appropriate action for the sabbath day?

6. When you think of being set free from that which binds you, what comes to your mind?

7. Reread verse 16. What do you think is the role of Satan in creating bondage?

What forms does that bondage take in our world today?

8. In what ways do you see Jesus' authority in this incident?

9. What were the responses of the people who were present?

---

10. If you had been present, how do you think you would have responded? Explain your response.

---

11. What could you stop doing on the sabbath to express your freedom from bondage?

---

12. What activities might you do on the sabbath that express freedom?

Spend some time thanking God for the freedom you have received. Ask God to increase your ability to live in true freedom in Christ.

Now or Later

The letter of Paul to the Galatians addresses the human tendency to try to achieve righteousness—to earn God's love—by obeying rules. We have been freed in Jesus Christ, and we can rest in God's unconditional love for us. Read Galatians 3:1-14 (you may also want to read Galatians 5:1-26). Spend some time reflecting on any tendencies you have of trying to earn God's love through what you do. Imagine what it would be like to experience a sabbath day where you rest in the reality that nothing you do can change God's amazing love for you.

8

The Gift of Grace

Ephesians 2:1-10

*The sabbath expresses the heart of the good news,
that God in Christ reveals an infinite love for us that does not depend
on our works. It depends simply on our willingness for it. . . .
What better way to reveal God's love beyond our works than to stop
our usual works and discover that love is not withdrawn but strongly
visible for us? Not only is this a witness for ourselves but also for
others as they see us intentionally celebrating an identity and love that
is not dependent on our worthy productions.*

TILDEN EDWARDS

Ann has been keeping sabbath for many years. Her experience on the sabbath involves stepping outside her life identity and living for one day as nothing but a child of God. She says that being a child of God, and only a child of God, on the sabbath is like slipping with relief into old, comfortable clothes. On the sabbath she is a disciple, not a leader. On the sabbath she is beloved, simply beloved. She began to keep the sabbath because she read some of the wonderful promises associated with the sabbath in Isaiah 58. She has continued to observe the sabbath because she has experienced it as one of her greatest joys, as a place where she experiences the great and wonderful grace of God.

GROUP DISCUSSION. On a piece of paper, write down the names of people you felt you had to please when you were a child. Describe to the group one of these people and how it felt when you tried to please him or her.

PERSONAL REFLECTION. Consider the people you felt you had to please when you were a child. In what ways were you able to please them? In what ways were you not able to please them? Now take a few moments to reflect: In what ways have you carried over anything from those relationships into your relationship with God?

This passage presents a strong "before and after" picture of what Christ has done for us. *Read Ephesians 2:1-10.*

---

1. In verses 1-3, what are the characteristics of people before they meet Christ?

---

2. What are the aspects of the way of life without Christ that make us dead?

---

3. In your heart of hearts, do you believe your life would be meaningless without God? Why or why not?

---

4. What do the words *mercy* and *grace* mean to you?

5. Verses 6 and 7 use rich language to describe the results of being made alive with Christ. Which words do you need to hear today, and why?

6. In verses 8 and 9, what is the contrast between faith and works?

7. In what ways do you find yourself falling into the belief that you can earn God's approval?

8. Since we were created for good works (v. 10), what makes it possible for these good works to flow from God's grace rather than being a way to earn God's love?

9. In your life, what are the settings and situations where you find it easiest to believe you are loved unconditionally by God?

What are the settings and situations where it is hard to believe God loves you?

10. The sabbath is a day to rest in God's grace. How might this affect your practice of sabbath?

---

11. If you have experimented with various forms of sabbath keeping during this study, or if you already have a sabbath practice, in what ways have your sabbath practices enabled you to experience God's grace?

---

12. Look back over these eight studies on the sabbath and consider what you might like to do or not do on the sabbath. If possible, make a commitment to try a few new practices for three to six months before reevaluating.

Spend some time thanking God for grace. Take some deep breaths and try to rest in the reality that you are loved no matter what you do. Ask God to help you receive his grace.

Now or Later

Psalm 103 expresses God's love and care for us and describes God's role as our redeemer. Read Psalm 103 twice slowly. The first time, observe all the ways God cares for us. The second time, pray the words of the psalm, praising God for his amazing love and grace. Spend some time praying or journaling about the connection between the sabbath and grace. In what ways can you grow in resting in grace on the sabbath?

Leader's Notes

Leading a Bible discussion can be an enjoyable and rewarding experience. But it can also be *scary*—especially if you've never done it before. If this is your feeling, you're in good company. When God asked Moses to lead the Israelites out of Egypt, he replied, "O LORD, please send someone else to do it" (Ex 4:13). It was the same with Solomon, Jeremiah and Timothy, but God helped these people in spite of their weaknesses, and he will help you as well.

You don't need to be an expert on the Bible or a trained teacher to lead a Bible discussion. The idea behind these inductive studies is that the leader guides group members to discover for themselves what the Bible has to say. This method of learning will allow group members to remember much more of what is said than a lecture would.

These studies are designed to be led easily. As a matter of fact, the flow of questions through the passage from observation to interpretation to application is so natural that you may feel that the studies lead themselves. This study guide is also flexible. You can use it with a variety of groups— student, professional, neighborhood or church groups. Each study takes forty-five to sixty minutes in a group setting.

There are some important facts to know about group dynamics and encouraging discussion. The suggestions listed below should enable you to effectively and enjoyably fulfill your role as leader.

Preparing for the Study

1. Ask God to help you understand and apply the passage in your own life. Unless this happens, you will not be prepared to lead others. Pray too for the various members of the group. Ask God to open your hearts to the message of his Word and motivate you to action.

2. Read the introduction to the entire guide to get an overview of the entire book and the issues which will be explored.

3. As you begin each study, read and reread the assigned Bible passage to familiarize yourself with it.

4. This study guide is based on the New International Version of the Bible. It will help you and the group if you use this translation as the basis for your study and discussion.

5. Carefully work through each question in the study. Spend time in meditation and reflection as you consider how to respond.

6. Write your thoughts and responses in the space provided in the study guide. This will help you to express your understanding of the passage clearly.

7. It might help to have a Bible dictionary handy. Use it to look up any unfamiliar words, names or places. (For additional help on how to study a passage, see chapter five of *How to Lead a LifeBuilder Study*, IVP, 2018.)

8. Consider how you can apply the Scripture to your life. Remember that the group will follow your lead in responding to the studies. They will not go any deeper than you do.

9. Once you have finished your own study of the passage, familiarize yourself with the leader's notes for the study you are leading. These are designed to help you in several ways. First, they tell you the purpose the study guide author had in mind when writing the study. Take time to think through how the study questions work together to accomplish that purpose. Second, the notes provide you with additional background information or suggestions on group dynamics for various questions. This information can be useful when people have difficulty understanding or answering a question. Third, the leader's notes can alert you to potential problems you may encounter during the study.

10. If you wish to remind yourself of anything mentioned in the leader's notes, make a note to yourself below that question in the study.

Leading the Study

1. Begin the study on time. Open with prayer, asking God to help the group to understand and apply the passage.

2. Be sure that everyone in your group has a study guide. Encourage the group to prepare beforehand for each discussion by reading the introduction to the guide and by working through the questions in the study.

3. At the beginning of your first time together, explain that these studies are meant to be discussions, not lectures. Encourage the members of the group to participate. However, do not put pressure on those who may be hesitant to speak during the first few sessions. You may want to suggest the following guidelines to your group.

☐ Stick to the topic being discussed.

☐ Your responses should be based on the verses which are the focus of the discussion and not on outside authorities such as commentaries or speakers. These studies focus on a particular passage of Scripture. Only rarely should you refer to other portions of the Bible. This allows for everyone to participate in in-depth study on equal ground.

☐ Anything said in the group is considered confidential and will not be discussed outside the group unless specific permission is given to do so.

☐ We will listen attentively to each other and provide time for each person present to talk.

☐ We will pray for each other.

4. Have a group member read the introduction at the beginning of the discussion.

5. Every session begins with a group discussion question. The question or activity is meant to be used before the passage is read. The question introduces the theme of the study and encourages group members to begin to open up. Encourage as many members as possible to participate, and be ready to get the discussion going with your own response.

This section is designed to reveal where our thoughts or feelings need to be transformed by Scripture. That is why it is especially important not to read the passage before the discussion question is asked. The passage will tend to color the honest reactions people would otherwise give because they are, of course, supposed to think the way the Bible does.

You may want to supplement the group discussion question with an ice-breaker to help people to get comfortable. See the community section of the *Small Group Starter Kit* (IVP, 1995) for more ideas.

You also might want to use the personal reflection question with your group. Either allow a time of silence for people to respond individually or discuss it together.

6. Have a group member (or members if the passage is long) read aloud the passage to be studied. Then give people several minutes to read the passage again silently so that they can take it all in.

7. Question 1 will generally be an overview question designed to briefly survey the passage. Encourage the group to look at the whole passage, but try to avoid getting sidetracked by questions or issues that will be addressed later in the study.

8. As you ask the questions, keep in mind that they are designed to be used just as they are written. You may simply read them aloud. Or you may prefer to express them in your own words.

There may be times when it is appropriate to deviate from the study guide. For example, a question may have already been answered. If so, move on to the next question. Or someone may raise an important question not covered in the guide. Take time to discuss it, but try to keep the group from going off on tangents.

9. Avoid answering your own questions. If necessary, repeat or rephrase them until they are clearly understood. Or point out something you read in the leader's notes to clarify the context or meaning. An eager group quickly becomes passive and silent if they think the leader will do most of the talking.

10. Don't be afraid of silence. People may need time to think about the question before formulating their answers.

11. Don't be content with just one answer. Ask, "What do the rest of you think?" or "Anything else?" until several people have given answers to the question.

12. Acknowledge all contributions. Try to be affirming whenever possible. Never reject an answer. If it is clearly off-base, ask, "Which verse led you to that conclusion?" or again, "What do the rest of you think?"

13. Don't expect every answer to be addressed to you, even though this will probably happen at first. As group members become more at ease, they will begin to truly interact with each other. This is one sign of healthy discussion.

14. Don't be afraid of controversy. It can be very stimulating. If you don't resolve an issue completely, don't be frustrated. Move on and keep it in mind for later. A subsequent study may solve the problem.

15. Periodically summarize what the group has said about the passage. This helps to draw together the various ideas mentioned and gives continuity to the study. But don't preach.

16. At the end of the Bible discussion you may want to allow group members a time of quiet to work on an idea under "Now or Later." Then discuss what you experienced. Or you may want to encourage group members to work on these ideas between meetings. Give an opportunity during the session for people to talk about what they are learning.

17. Conclude your time together with conversational prayer, adapting the prayer suggestion at the end of the study to your group. Ask for God's help in following through on the commitments you've made.

18. End on time.

Many more suggestions and helps are found in *How to Lead a LifeBuilder Study*.

Components of Small Groups

A healthy small group should do more than study the Bible. There are four components to consider as you structure your time together.

Nurture. Small groups help us to grow in our knowledge and love of God. Bible study is the key to making this happen and is the foundation of your small group.

Community. Small groups are a great place to develop deep friendships with other Christians. Allow time for informal interaction before and after each study. Plan activities and games that will help you get to know each other. Spend time having fun together—going on a picnic or cooking dinner together.

Worship and prayer. Your study will be enhanced by spending time praising God together in prayer or song. Pray for each other's needs—and keep track of how God is answering prayer in your group. Ask God to help you to apply what you are learning in your study.

Outreach. Reaching out to others can be a practical way of applying what you are learning, and it will keep your group from becoming self-focused. Host a series of evangelistic discussions for your friends or neighbors. Clean up the yard of an elderly friend. Serve at a soup kitchen together, or spend a day working in the community.

Many more suggestions and helps in each of these areas are found in the *Small Group Starter Kit*. You will also find information on building a small group. Reading through the starter kit will be worth your time.

Study 1. An Invitation to Relax in Abundance.
Genesis 1:1—2:3.

Purpose: To see the ways sabbath observance flows from God's abundant and well-ordered creation.

Group discussion. Be sure to have pieces of paper and pencils or pens for the participants to use. You'll need paper and pens for the group discussion portions of a number of the studies in this guide.

Personal reflection. If you are studying in a group, you can skip these questions or you can include them as a time for individual reflection. Allow a period of silence for people to reflect on the things that impede their experience of God's goodness and generosity. Then invite them to talk about their thoughts if they want to.

Question 3. In addition to the repeated words in the descriptions of each of the days of creation, scholars note that the pattern of light, waters and dry land in days one to three is repeated in days four through six. In days one through three, light is *created* first, then water, then dry land. On the fourth day the lights are *organized* into sun, moon and stars; on the fifth day the waters *bring forth* sea creatures (as well as birds); and on the sixth day the earth (the dry land) *brings forth* creatures.

Question 4. The description of what happens on the sixth day is much longer than for the other days. The creation of the animals is described with a fair amount of detail, and the creation of humans has many unique characteristics. Unlike the other parts of creation, the humans are created in the image of God, and they are given dominion over creation and a mandate to fill the earth and care for it. In addition, God speaks directly to the humans, something he has not done to any other parts of the created world, affirming that there is the possibility of intimate relationship between the Creator and these humans he just created. These unique aspects of the day are some of the possible reasons why God uses the words "very good" (in contrast with "good" on the other days) to describe what occurs on the sixth day.

Question 6. The sabbath is a day to remember the abundance of creation and be thankful: "We focus less on our lack, and more on our abundance. As we do, our thirst and hunger for more than we need begins to fall away. In quiet stillness we can identify our genuine needs with more precision, and separate them more easily from our mindless wants and desires" (Wayne Muller, *Sabbath* [New York: Bantam, 1999], p. 127).

Question 8. The word *rest* in these verses comes from the same root as "sabbath." "In a delightful twist, 'rest' is a verb in this passage and 'work' is a noun. Sabbath rest is active, not passive. Furthermore, it has meaning only in reference to God's creative work. Sabbath rest is not the absence of work. It is work's fulfillment. It celebrates creative labor. Rather than saying 'no' to work, sabbath says 'enough for now'" (Richard Lowery, *Sabbath and Jubilee* [St. Louis: Chalice Press, 2000], p. 93).

Question 9. People often wonder if God rested at creation because he was tired. God rests not because he is tired but because rest is a sign of completion and abundance. The universe is so well-ordered, and God's gifts to humanity are so generous and good, that God is able to rest. God invites us to enter into his rest as a sign that we acknowledge that everything good comes from God. Our rest shows that we depend completely on the God who created and sustains us.

Question 10. *Holiness* in the Old and New Testaments has two aspects to its meaning: separate and pure. The word is applied in the Old Testament to places, things, seasons and people who have been appointed to lead the people in worship. But most of all, the word refers to God and God's character. "One of the most distinguished words in the Bible is the word *qadosh*, holy; a word which more than any other is representative of the mystery and majesty of the divine. Now what was the first holy object in the history of the world? Was it a mountain? Was it an altar? . . . How extremely significant is the fact that it is applied to time: 'And God blessed the seventh day and made it holy'" (Abraham Heschel, *The Sabbath* [New York: Farrar, Straus and Giroux, 1951], p. 9).

According to Celeste Perrino Walker in *Making Sabbath Special* ([Nampa, Id.: Pacific Press, 1999], p. 17), the word *blessed* in the Bible, when applied to God, communicates praise. When applied to humans and human life, *blessed* has the sense of happy. In the Old Testament, the sabbath functioned as a sign of God's blessing.

Question 11. "Most of us seem to have an ambivalent relationship with the idea of rest. We feel guilty about doing 'nothing' and resting before we've cleared up things in the world. Many of us exhibit a drivenness that implies on the one hand an anxious over-valuing of our own individual actions for the welfare of the world, and on the other hand, a lack of trust that God is also working in a much larger framework for wholeness and justice. The idea of Sabbath resting in prayer runs counter to the whole mentality of the Protestant work ethic with which many of us have been raised" (Ron Farr, "Sabbath Resting in God," *Weavings Journal*, March/April 1993, p. 23).

Question 12. Here are a couple good ideas about how to keep sabbath: "Good sabbath-keeping includes praying and playing. Prayerful sabbaths without play or playful sabbath without prayer are only half-sabbaths. Prayer without play can degenerate into a dutiful but cheerless religion. Play without prayer can become mind-numbing escape" (Don Postema, *Catch Your Breath* [Grand Rapids: CRC Publications, 1997], p. 71).

"[Sabbath] is a time for 'useless' poetry and other arts; a time to appreciate a tree, your neighbor, and yourself without doing something to them; a time to praise God as an end in itself. It is a time for superfluous—overflowing the merely necessary—movements, meetings and words" (Tilden Edwards, *Sabbath Time* [Nashville: Upper Room, 2003], p. 103).

Study 2. Choosing to Stop Working. Exodus 16:1-30.
Purpose: To explore what it looks like and feels like to stop working for a day.
Personal reflection. You may want to allow people a few moments of silence to think about the place of being productive in their lives.

Question 3. We often believe that all grumbling or complaining is wrong. In this story, God responds to the complaints of the Israelites by promising to meet the need for food that they have expressed. God does not seem to be angry about this expression of a genuine need. In this story, God seems more angry about the Israelites' failure to obey his command regarding sabbath food gathering (verses 28 and 29). It appears from this story that perhaps grumbling and complaining are not offensive in God's eyes when a genuine need is present, and that God delights to meet our real needs.

Question 7. There are many reasons why people find it difficult to stop working. The momentum of activity is one reason: "There is a terrific amount of momentum in our lives like that of a freight train, relentlessly driving us and keeping us from resting in the present moment. We feel inwardly compelled to be productive, to be responsible, to be on time, to make a good impression, to be liked or needed, to make our mark, to reform that in the world which offends our sense of justice. . . . The freight train of our restless minds and hearts is not easily stopped. And we're not always sure we want to stop it" (Farr, "Sabbath Resting in God," p. 23).

A second reason we find it difficult to stop working is that we humans often fight the idea that rest is good for us. Wayne Muller, in *Sabbath*, points out that many plants and animals experience periods of dormancy. Many fruit trees, for example, must lie dormant during winter in order to bear fruit the next season. He calls dormancy a "spiritual and biological necessity" (p. 7), and believes that when we do not have periods of dormancy in our lives we will experience confusion and erosion of energy.

Question 9. In the Jewish tradition, according to Abraham Heschel, the sabbath helps us celebrate God's presence in time rather than space. During our work days, we focus on things that occupy space. On the sabbath, we try to get in touch with holiness in time, the eternal.

Question 10. Stopping our productivity on the sabbath can help us remember God is the one who provides for us. This rest does not indicate that work doesn't matter, it is simply a part of finding a balance point. When we have experienced enough rest, we are able to work with enthusiasm and joy, and we are more likely to experience God's presence and guidance as we work.

Allow a few minutes in silent reflection before you ask the group to respond to the second part of this question.

Question 11. As we will see in the next study, many sabbath keepers enjoy getting out in nature on their sabbath. The beauty and complexity of God's creation can remind us that God is our provider. In addition, prayers of thankfulness on the sabbath can help us focus on all the things God does in our lives and God's many gifts and blessings to us, which remind us that we don't generate the good things in our lives.

Study 3. Finding Refreshment in God's Creation. Exodus 20:1-21.
Purpose: To explore the reason given in God's command to keep the sabbath and to discuss the impact of that reason in our lives today.
Question 3. In the Old Testament, *holy* means both separate and pure. We tend to think of holiness solely as moral purity, and God's moral purity is indeed one way he is separate from us. However, God's holiness—his separateness from us—is much more than his moral purity: God is powerful in ways that we are not, his love is unconditional unlike ours, he is the Creator and we are creatures, and so on. Thinking about keeping the sabbath "holy" only in the sense of moral purity can make people think they should not have fun. After participants share the ways they understand the word *holy,* mention that in the Old Testament *holy* also means "separate." Ask participants to describe how that definition changes their understanding of how the sabbath might be holy.

Drawing on the meaning of *holy* as "separate," encourage participants to consider activities that help them step aside from their everyday lives. Holiness is not a super-spiritual state of purity; it reflects the call to be set apart for God. We can bring God's holiness into our everyday lives through many different spiritual disciplines such as intercessory prayer, contemplative prayer, Bible study, caring for people in need and loving our families.
Question 4. In many translations, such as the New International Version and the New Revised Standard Version, the two words used in the sabbath command are "work" and "labor." They are basically synonyms, but people in the group may give different nuances to the two words. For some people, "work" is a positive activity and "labor" captures the toil and pain of work. For some people who don't work for pay, "labor" helps them consider the kinds of work they do around the house. This question gets at the variety of emotions we experience when we consider our work life, and it sets the stage for the next question, where we consider the variety of things we consider to be work.
Question 5. The fire command has particular significance for women and slaves/servants, who used fire for cooking. Forbidding a fire helped to make certain that women and slaves/servants wouldn't work on the sabbath. Note that work is much more than what we do for pay. Students work when they study. Homemakers work when they clean, shop for food or do laundry. Retired people have regular tasks to do around the house, in the garden or in the community. Encourage participants to think broadly about what feels like

work to them.

"In the broad consensus of the tradition, what should not be done [on the sabbath] is 'work.' Defining exactly what that means is a long and continuing argument, but one classic answer is that work is whatever changes the natural, material world. All week long, human beings wrestle with the created world, tilling and hammering and carrying and burning. On the sabbath, however, Jews let it be. They celebrate it as it is and live in it in peace and gratitude. Humans are created too, after all. It is right and good to remember that it is not human effort alone that grows grain and forges steel" (Dorothy Bass, *Receiving the Day* [San Francisco: Jossey-Bass, 2000], p. 51).

"What is labor for some may be Sabbath rest for others. On our way to church we drive past a Laundromat. It is always busy, even on Sundays. That isn't my way to honor the Sabbath, but I have friends who have experienced the Laundromat as a pleasant getaway—a place to read, to chat with neighbors, to get away from the furor of a busy household. In the same vein, a 'Sunday painter' finds restoration and new life with an easel and canvas and brushes, while an artist who paints for a living would do well to close the door of the studio as a way of entering the Sabbath. A professional cook might choose to stay out of any kitchen, while for a bookkeeper or lawyer, cooking would be a true feast for the soul as well as the body" (Martha Hickman, *A Day of Rest* [New York: Avon Books, 1999], pp. 72-73).

Question 6. It would have been revolutionary in the ancient world for women and slaves/servants to have a day of rest along with the men. Thus the sabbath is a sign of God's care for the people on the margins, the people who are not powerful. It is equally striking that rest for farm animals is commanded. Humans, though important in the universe, are not the only focus of God's attention and care. All of creation exists in relationship with God and receives God's care.

Question 8. You may want to summarize some of the ideas discussed in study 1 when exploring the creation story.

Question 9. Several scholars have pointed out that, the Hebrew word for God's resting in the fourth commandment literally means "to catch one's breath." A fruitful sabbath discipline involves focusing on our breath. Taking a few deep breaths slows down the body and mind, which can be very helpful to promote a sense of resting in God's presence. Many Christians enjoy breath prayer, where they imagine themselves breathing in God's love and breathing out their cares and frustrations into God's presence. An ancient prayer that can be used as a breath prayer is: "Lord Jesus Christ, Son of God, have mercy on me, a sinner" (based on Lk 18:13). Say each phrase silently accompanied by one breath.

Question 10. We can stop some of the activities that enslave us and keep us out of touch with nature. This may include taking a break from the compulsion to answer e-mail, watch the TV news, play video games, surf the Internet or use household appliances.

Question 11. Many people who observe the sabbath talk about how much they enjoy getting out in nature on the sabbath: walking, riding bikes, playing Frisbee with a dog, or doing some gentle gardening. They report how much they enjoy noticing the beauty of nature, with all its colors, shapes and smells, and how refreshing it is to enjoy the movement of their physical bodies in God's created world.

Another way to enjoy nature is to focus on engaging the senses. Traditional Jewish sabbath activities involve singing a song with our mouths, smelling special bread baking, lighting candles, eating delicious food, and breathing the smell of sweet spices to mark the end of the sabbath. Many wonderful sensory experiences are close to us but on our work days we rush past them. The sabbath is a day to stop and enjoy them.

One more way to enjoy nature on the sabbath is to find ways to tread lightly on creation. Options include staying out of the car and fixing a meal made from organic foods. These activities allow nature to enjoy a sabbath rest along with humans.

Study 4. Discovering Sabbath Delight. Isaiah 58.

Purpose: To explore the connection between spiritual disciplines, such as sabbath observance, and the way we live our everyday lives.

General note. An old saying affirms that, more than the Jews have kept the sabbath, the sabbath has kept the Jews. The sabbath has sustained Jewish identity over the centuries. Therefore, Christians must honor the sabbath as belonging first of all to the Jews. Dorothy Bass suggests that we can do our best to learn from this Jewish practice in ways that are appropriate to our own faith. She writes that the sabbath sings the music of creation and liberation, themes that are appropriate for Christians as well as Jews (*Receiving the Day*, pp. 51-52).

Group discussion and personal reflection. The challenge in this discussion is that all disciplines, even very healthy disciplines, sometimes feel like we are "going through the motions." Sometimes we do them even though our heart isn't in them, but over time we usually reap great benefits from our good habits and disciplines if our hearts are in the right place enough of the time.

In this passage, though, we will see that we can go too far in the direction of going through the motions. Our hearts need to be engaged—as much of the time as possible—alongside our actions when we embrace a spiritual discipline. And our everyday lives need to reflect—as much as possible—our faith commitments.

Question 1. Almost all of the Old Testament prophets, at one time or another, condemn the people of Israel for disobedience to God's commands. This passage stands out because it emphasizes that external obedience in itself is not the point. Obedience needs to be part of a whole life that is dedicated to God's priorities.

Question 2. This view of fasting is unique in the Bible. Most fasting in the Bible is for mourning or repentance or to enhance prayer. Fasting as a way to loose the chains of injustice was adopted by the early church. In the first centuries after Christ, fasting was practiced as a way to free up food and money to give to the poor. As fasting is becoming more common now than it was in most of the twentieth century, Christians are rediscovering fasting as a way to experience solidarity with the poor, as well as to free up resources to give to the poor.

Question 7. "In the spiritual life, the word 'discipline' means 'the effort to create some space in which God can act.' Discipline means to prevent everything in your life from being filled up. Discipline means that somewhere you're not occupied, and certainly not preoccupied. In the spiritual life, discipline means to create that space in which something can happen that you hadn't planned on or counted on" (Henri Nouwen, quoted in *The Sacred Way* by Tony Jones [Grand Rapids: Zondervan: 2005], p. 32).

Questions 10-11. Many sabbath keepers turn off the television and the computer on the sabbath. Life on the screen seems to encourage us to be too self-focused and self-absorbed. We need a break from the advertisements on TV and the Internet, which encourage us toward consumerism and materialism—a break that will help us reconnect with God's values of justice and generosity to people in need.

Consider what symbols of faith give you delight. Jews use candles to begin and end the sabbath, and for many Christians, candles convey both delight and the light of God's presence. Jews end the sabbath by smelling spices, as a symbol of their desire that the sweetness of the sabbath would flavor the other days of the week. The sabbath may be a day to get out a potpourri of spices to flavor the air with sweetness.

Some people, particularly single people, need to consider how to create sabbath delight in the presence of friends. Some of us find it difficult to rest because it means being alone. Sometimes the attraction of the workplace and the marketplace is the bustle of shared activity. Saying "I like to keep busy" is not necessarily a sign of being a workaholic. Instead it can represent the joy of being with others. One of the opportunities that the sabbath brings is to join with others in hikes, bike rides, walks, games and relaxed conversations.

Study 5. A Gift for Us. Mark 2:23-28.

Purpose: To compare and contrast Jesus' and the Pharisees' views of the sabbath so that we can discover the true purpose of sabbath disciplines.

General note. "The dispute between Jesus and his rabbinical opponents is not whether to observe sabbath, but how to observe it. The Pharisees apparently interpret the disciples' plucking of grain in the light of Exodus 34:21, which explicitly forbids agricultural work on the sabbath. . . . The more fitting association, however, is with the gleaning tradition. . . . Jesus' disciples pluck grain, not as householders who own the crop and have the right to sell it, but as the economically vulnerable who have a God-given right to take what they need to survive" (Lowery, *Sabbath and Jubilee*, p. 128).

Question 2. By the time of Jesus, the sabbath had become one of the distinguishing characteristics of the Jewish people. Jewish texts from around Jesus' time prohibited thirty-nine specific activities on the sabbath, including grinding, kneading, baking, spinning, weaving, hunting, slaughtering, building, hammering and transporting. Two of the thirty-nine forbidden activities were reaping and threshing. In this story, Jesus' disciples were reaping and threshing, admittedly on a very small scale, but the Jewish sabbath regulations of Jesus' time were clear that these activities were not to be done at all.

Question 4. Ethicists have debated for centuries about the delicate balance point between meeting human needs and obeying laws and rules. A discussion of this question could last for hours. Keep the discussion of this question fairly short, but do allow people to express their opinions briefly. Answering this question will help people in the group get to know each other better, because it taps into deeply held values that we seldom have the opportunity to express.

Question 5. A fairly close parallel to the Jewish sabbath in Jesus' time was the sabbath practice of the Puritans, which continued to influence life in the United States through the first half of the twentieth century. The Puritans' view of the sabbath was very legalistic. Because play could degenerate into debauchery, they banned anything resembling play on the sabbath and emphasized being serious. This ruled out the life-giving aspects of imagination, intuition and creativity.

Question 6. "Perhaps the word which best summarizes what God offers us through the gift of rest is 'balance.' Our lives get lopsided when they are too stuffed with activity, so packed down with things to do that we have no time to be" (Elizabeth Canham, "A Rest Remaining," *Weavings Journal,* March/April 1993, p. 30).

Question 8. The gleaning tradition in the Old Testament allowed the poor to harvest what they needed from the edges of landowners' fields and from anything that was left after the harvest (Lev 19:9-10; 23:22, Deut 24:19-21; Ruth 2). Jesus seems to be drawing on the gleaning tradition as he reframed the purpose of the sabbath in this story.

Question 9. "He who wants to enter the holiness of the day must first lay down the profanity of clattering commerce, of being yoked to toil. He must go away from the screech of dissonant days, from the nervousness and fury of acquisitiveness. . . . He must say farewell to manual work and learn to understand that the world has already been created and will survive without the help of man. Six days a week we wrestle with the world, wringing profit from the earth; on the Sabbath we especially care for the seed of eternity planted in the soul. The world has our hands, but our soul belongs to Someone Else" (Heschel, *Sabbath,* p. 13).

Question 10. Stopping work on the sabbath out of obedience to God, even when the tasks that need to be done seem compelling and urgent, can be a definite sign of submission to Jesus as Lord, a manifestation of our belief that Jesus knows us better than we know ourselves.

Question 11. Attending church, reading the Bible, praying prayers of thankfulness, showing love to friends or family members can all be signs of our submission to Jesus as Lord. For many people, being in nature is a reminder that Jesus is Lord of creation—and Lord of everything—which puts our lives and our commitments into perspective. Taking a nap on the sabbath can be an affirmation that Jesus rules the universe and we do not; therefore we can relax in peace. These activities can be done in a spirit of uncomfortable duty or mindless recreation, but they can also be done with joy and gladness on the sabbath, as a reflection of Christ's lordship.

These questions may raise a related question: What is the dividing line between being selfish and resting in God's goodness on the sabbath? Longtime sabbath observers know that this is a real question with no easy answers. Each person has to wrestle with this question before God. An important goal for sabbath keeping is to let go of perfectionism for the day, which includes letting go of the illusion that we can somehow make our sabbaths perfect. Sometimes our rest will be too selfish, and we will need to rediscover ways to keep God's goodness and grace at the center of the day. Sometimes we will try to be perfectionists on our day of rest, attempting to observe a sabbath day that is spiritual in every way, and we will need to let go of the need to prove that we can do things perfectly. Over time, with adjustments and flexibility, we will find a grace-filled balance point.

Study 6. We Are Valuable. Matthew 12:9-14.

Purpose: To discover how sabbath can help us view ourselves through God's eyes.

Question 1. As we saw in the previous study, in Jesus' time the Pharisees accepted the teaching of the rabbis that thirty-nine activities—all of them describing types of work—were forbidden on the sabbath. The specific nature of the activities on the list made it easy for the Pharisees to catch Jesus and his disciplines violating the rules. Jesus seemed to be very intentional in his violation of those rules for another set of values regarding appropriate sabbath activities. So the sabbath was a place where the Jewish authorities could easily confront Jesus, something they seemed eager to do whenever possible.

Question 2. The man is present in the synagogue when Jesus enters. His presence there is significant, first, because it indicates something about his connection to his community and/or his faith in God. He could have nurtured bitterness about his withered hand and felt motivated to withdraw from his community of faith. He could have been angry at God about his hand and stayed away from worship in the synagogue. But evidently he did not respond in either of those ways. The second significant thing we can observe about the man is that when Jesus asked him to stretch out his hand, he obeyed. He could have argued with Jesus or refused to move his hand. His obedience to Jesus' words indicates, at the very least, some basic level of trust in Jesus.

Question 3. The Pharisees question Jesus about the lawfulness of healing on the sabbath, indicating the priority they placed on the law over human needs. After the healing, the Pharisees left and began to conspire to destroy him. Mostly likely these priorities would have been visible in their faces, words, body language and tones of voice.

Question 4. Many sabbath keepers don't get too worried if some unplanned work has to be done—briefly!—on the sabbath. However, if unplanned work cuts into the restfulness of the day week after week, then some reevaluation needs to be done. Perhaps we are letting things slide the other six days so we will have an excuse to work on the sabbath. We have to be careful not to set up rigid rules for the sabbath, but we also have to be careful not to deceive ourselves into letting work creep into the day.

Question 5. The man's ailment, the shriveling of his hand, was not urgent in the sense that the man might die if he wasn't healed that day. This is true of all of Jesus' healings on the sabbath; he never healed anyone with an emergency medical need. Would a sheep die if it fell in a pit and was left there until the next day? Probably not, but the sheep would be very distressed. Most shepherds would have compassion for the sheep and lift it out. Jesus seemed to be making a point about compassion being at the heart of the sabbath rather than slavish obedience to rules.

Question 6. One goal for the sabbath may be "to free up some time to perform some act of mercy—a visit to a sick person, some talk on the phone with a friend who needs us" (Hickman, *A Day of Rest,* p. 68).

Question 7. Humans alone of all creation are created in God's image (Gen 1:26). Therefore humans have a special place in creation, yet humans also have a responsibility to care for creation as God's stewards (Gen 1:26, 28). This acknowledges that all creatures have value and should be cared for because they were made by God.

Question 10. Many people find that media distort their view of themselves as beloved children of God. Whether it's TV or magazine advertisements with ridiculously beautiful models, sitcoms or novels that promote laissez-faire sexuality, movies or TV shows with fantasy plots, media can play a part in encouraging us to view ourselves as falling short in some way.

Question 11. One mother found that the stress of countering her children's negative comments was wearing her down and making her begin to think negative thoughts. She suggested that the family's sabbath observance might include trying to avoid complaining. She found that her children's friends enjoyed coming to her house on Sundays because they found it so enjoyable to be in a complaint-free zone for a few hours.

Study 7. Freed from Bondage. Luke 13:10-17.

Purpose: To explore the ways the sabbath is a day to celebrate freedom from bondage.

General note. The nature of this woman's ailment is a symbol of being oppressed or burdened. She is bent over as if bearing a yoke. Jesus reminds his opponents and followers that they release their yoked animals on the sabbath, and he encourages a view of the sabbath as a day of release for a yoked and bound daughter of Abraham. Richard Lowery, in *Sabbath and Jubilee*, points out that his opponents are shamed by Jesus' words because they have missed the fundamental point that the sabbath, at its heart, is a day of release from bondage (p. 135).

Question 2. We also saw in the previous lesson that the Pharisees gave priority to the law over human need. Here we see that priority articulated even more clearly.

Question 3. Jesus' authority threatened the Jewish leaders on several levels. On the one hand, he broke the sabbath laws of the time and seemed utterly confident that God wanted him to do so. His confidence and the way he argued his points and engaged the crowds confounded the Pharisees. His ability to heal would have frustrated them in an even deeper way. Healing reveals a kind of power that is utterly baffling to people who believe God's highest call is to obey rules and laws. In verse 14 the Pharisees say they wish he would heal on another day, but most likely they would have preferred that he not heal anyone at any time.

Question 5. The connection between freedom and the sabbath dates back to the very first sabbath observance in the Old Testament, which we looked at in study 2 (Ex 16:1-30). The second version of the sabbath commandment in the Ten Commandments in Deuteronomy 5:12-15, which was suggested in study 3 for "Now or Later," also emphasizes freedom as a central motivation for sabbath observance. Both of these Old Testament passages encourage the people to remember God's miraculous action in freeing the people of Israel from slavery in Egypt. The Jewish leaders of Jesus' time set up sabbath rules and structures in order to allow people to celebrate freedom from work, but the rigid rules seem to have diminished the sense of freedom on the sabbath day.

Question 7. Christians vary on whether they view Satan as an evil person who desires to lead them astray or as an impersonal force for evil. The Bible could be used to support either view. Either way, there is no doubt that evil forces are at work in our world creating bondage, pain and suffering for people.

Bondage today includes many forms of addiction, including addiction to substances and addiction to productivity, consumerism and materialism. In addition, many people are unable to enjoy quiet rest. We are so used to the stimuli of the world around us that being quiet can feel unnatural, unfamiliar and even threatening. One of the gifts of the sabbath over time is an increasing comfort with slowing down and silence.

When we consider the kind of freedom we can experience and celebrate on the sabbath, we need to be careful not to slip into the belief that healthy sabbath observance will heal deep-seated addictions. Over time, sabbath observance is definitely healing; it brings health and balance to our tendency to base our self-worth in productivity. And a restful sabbath may make us less susceptible to the power of consumerism and materialism because we can grow in seeing what really matters in life. But for addictions like alcoholism, drug abuse and gambling, medical and/or psychological treatment is necessary.

Question 11. What do you find it hard to stop doing? Worrying? Being angry? On the sabbath we can structure our day, as well as our thoughts, to reduce worrying and anger. Dorothy Bass, in *Receiving the Day*, talks about choosing not to engage in activities that will summon worry, such as paying bills, doing tax returns, making "to do" lists, and thinking about people who make us angry (p. 65). This is only one aspect of the freedom Christ intends for us, which includes much broader and deeper things as well, but these small freedoms, practiced over time, can teach us about the larger freedom Christ gives us.

Question 12. Consider the kinds of activities that communicate joy and celebration. Humans, whether people of faith or not, have an innate desire to celebrate. Christians have so much to celebrate: what God has done, what God is doing, and what God will do in the future. This Good News lies at the heart of a Christian sabbath celebration.

Study 8. The Gift of Grace. Ephesians 2:1-10.

Purpose: To explore the ways the sabbath enables us to experience God's grace.

Question 4. According to the *New Bible Dictionary,* in the Greek of the New Testament "mercy" refers to compassion to someone in need, distress or debt (p. 751). "Grace" refers to good will or favor. These definitions are very similar to the way the words are used in contemporary English. The concept of grace has a prominent place in the writings of the apostle Paul, who argues that because of God's grace, we are treated as if we had never sinned, even though we are guilty (pp. 433-34).

Question 6. "Our identity and dignity are given by the God who created and redeemed us. We do not work to merit salvation. It is given to us" (Postema, *Catch Your Breath,* p. 66).

Question 7. Some people may be tempted to observe the sabbath in order to make God love them more. "On the Sabbath we are not to do any work or to employ others to work for us. It is a miserable and hopeless business to obey this commandment with the goal of securing God's love and favor by doing so. . . . If you expect to climb to a higher position in God's appreciation by Sabbath observance you are apt to experience frustration and dismay. The Sabbath will be no delight to you if you keep it out of fear that God will do dreadful things to you if you do not comply with his law" (Walter Chantry, *Call the Sabbath a Delight* [Carlisle, Penn.: Banner of Truth Trust, 1991], p. 78).

Question 8. The Holy Spirit works in us to transform us. Sometimes the Spirit's work is instant and immediate, bringing changes that can be seen from one day to the next. Sometimes the Spirit works over time, bringing gradual change that comes as we love and obey God and seek to serve God. The Holy Spirit—sometimes instantly and sometimes over time—increases our joy in obeying God and gives us the ability to let our actions flow out of our love for God. Romans 8 and Galatians 5 are excellent resources for understanding this work of the Holy Spirit in our lives and for getting a picture of what it looks like to do good things that flow from our love of God.

Question 9. Wayne Muller, in *Sabbath*, points out that one of the astonishing aspects of the sabbath is its total uselessness. Nothing productive will get done, no goals will be met, and nothing will get checked of a list. Sabbath activities are completely without measurable value. Muller believes that many of us find it difficult to slow our pace because we feel a strong need to be useful (p. 211).

Question 10. Celeste Perrino Walker, in *Making Sabbath Special*, notes that we have three things to celebrate on the sabbath: God made us and the rest of creation with care and love, God has redeemed us through Jesus Christ, and one day God will restore all things on earth and in heaven. She believes that we can structure a sabbath celebration around these three joyous truths (p. 29).

Many writers emphasize that the most significant thing we can do on the sabbath to experience God's grace is to limit our activities and simply enjoy resting and slowing down. This enables us to experience the reality that we are valued not for what we accomplish but because God loves us unconditionally. Wayne Muller makes the comparison with an unborn child in the womb, who receives an endless supply of warmth, nourishment and protection simply because of being there, not because of anything he or she has done to deserve that care. He suggests that in the same way, during sabbath time, "does the sweet womb of rest enfold us, nourish us, heal and restore us" (*Sabbath*, p. 212).

Question 12. Many people who begin keeping sabbath are tempted to take on too much. It is enough to begin by stopping one to three activities on the sabbath. It is enough to pick one to three things to do on the sabbath. Another temptation is to keep the sabbath one time and then start evaluating. If you desire to begin a sabbath practice, make a plan and follow it for three to six months, or perhaps even a year. Resist the temptation to analyze during that period; simply receive the gift of the sabbath. Wait until the end of that time and then reflect on what you have experienced. Let the sabbath teach you.

Lynne M. Baab, Ph.D., is a Presbyterian minister. She served in pastoral roles in two Seattle congregations before moving to New Zealand to teach pastoral theology at the University of Otago. She returned to Seattle in 2017.

Printed and bound by CPI Group (UK) Ltd, Croydon, CR0 4YY

13/04/2025

14656475-0001